Voices from the American Revolution

SPEECHMAKERS
& WRITERS

David Haugen, Book Editor

BLACKBIRCH®
PRESS

THOMSON

GALE

San Diego • Detroit • New York • San Francisco • Cleveland • New Haven, Conn. • Waterville, Maine • London • Munich

LIBRARY OF CONGRESS CATALOGING-IN-PUBLICATION DATA

Speechmakers and Writers / by David Haugen
    p. cm. — (Voices from the American Revolution)
Summary: A history of the Revolutionary War, as told through diary excerpts, letters,
and personal narratives from writers, speechmakers, and other eyewitnesses.
Includes index.
  ISBN 1-4103-0415-9 (lib. bdg. : alk. paper)

CONTENTS

A WAR OF WORDS AND IDEAS

J uly 5, 1776—the day after the Continental Congress approved the
Declaration of Independence—newspapers and colonial spokesmen began
spreading the word that America was officially fighting for its freedom from
England. Throughout the villages and military camps around Philadelphia, where
Congress had met, speakers read the entire declaration to anxious crowds. Within the
first paragraph of their recitations, these men uttered the famous lines, "We hold
these truths to be self-evident, that all men are created equal, that they are endowed
by their Creator with certain unalienable Rights, that among these are Life, Liberty,
and the pursuit of Happiness." Written by Thomas Jefferson, then a Virginia lawyer
and delegate to Congress, these few words expressed the basic ideals that character-
ized America's struggle for independence. The colonial rebels believed their
"unalienable" rights—those rights that cannot be taken away from an individual—
were being ignored by the British government. The rebels, therefore, assumed they
had just cause to declare their independence from England's tyrannical rule.

The Declaration of Independence is the best illustration that the Revolutionary
War (1775–1783) was a battle not only of soldiers and weapons but also of words and
ideas. In fact, the declaration was the peak of this revolutionary contest. For more
than a decade before that famous July 4, several British colonists in America had
become dissatisfied with England's treatment of the colonies. Britain's Parliament had
levied a series of taxes upon the colonies to help support England's sagging economy.
Many in the colonies believed such taxes were unfair since the colonials had no representative in Parliament. The colonists also assumed their own colonial governments
would best determine how the colonies should be taxed or otherwise managed. In

With the signing of the Declaration of Independence, the Continental Congress took the
greatest step toward showing Britain that America would go to war to win independence.

1765, Patrick Henry, a member of the colonial government of Virginia, made this argument when he wrote, "The General Assembly of this Colony have the only and sole exclusive Right and Power to lay Taxes and Impositions upon the Inhabitants of this Colony and that every Attempt to vest such Power in any Person or Persons whatsoever other than the General Assembly aforesaid has a manifest Tendency to destroy British as well as American Freedom." Henry's words, as well as those of many other patriots, made it clear that taxes or any other burdens placed upon the colonies would endanger the relationship between England and America and threaten colonial liberty.

In the decade between Patrick Henry's resolves and the first shots of the Revolutionary War, a host of speakers and idealists debated the justness of England's determination to rule its colonies as it saw fit. Not everyone in the colonies agreed that taxation, for example, was unfair. After all, the colonists were British subjects. Even many of the colonial leaders who resented the taxes enjoyed being part of the British Empire and wished to remain so. The rebellious elements in the colonies, however, were more vocal. Men like Patrick Henry and Samuel Adams argued that tolerating any form of tyranny would lead to slavery. They made speeches that captivated audiences and persuaded a growing number of colonists that the solution was not political reform but complete independence for America.

The arguments against taxation and even for independence were not put forth by unthinking men acting out revenge for England's wrongs. Patrick Henry and Thomas Jefferson, for example, were lawyers who had been educated in English law and the rights afforded to individuals under the English constitution. Before 1774—the year in which Parliament passed some of the harshest measures against the colonies— these men wrote or spoke out against the legal injustices of England's management of the colonies. Once it became clear that the Crown was ignoring the pleas of the colonists, men like Henry and Boston politician Samuel Adams put their fiery speaking skills to the task of promoting independence. Their endeavor was difficult, however, since many colonists did not agree that misguided policies were a cause for separation between England and America.

The same types of debates that flared in colonial towns were also taken up in Britain's Parliament. In the decade before the war, the right to tax the colonies was a controversial issue among the members of Parliament. When Prime Minister George Grenville announced the Stamp Act in 1765, he thought the burden would be light and inoffensive. He also believed that the colonies existed to benefit England. Such notions had been around at least since 1696 when Britain derived its Navigation Acts, a series of laws that declared that the colonies were mainly economic extensions of England. Many members of Parliament supported this view, but others did not. William Pitt warned that passing unpopular legislature such as the Stamp Act would eventually turn the colonies against England. Through a series of other taxes

Patrick Henry wrote that taxes and other restrictions imposed by the British government threatened the relationship between England and the colonies.

and hostile legislation, other members of Parliament took the side of the colonists. Edmund Burke argued that it was unfair to try to enforce legislation upon the colonies since Americans had no say in the government that was deciding colonial policies. While these voices of opposition denounced England's regulations, they stopped short of supporting the colonial bid for independence.

When the Declaration of Independence formally revealed America's war aim, the outcome of the Revolution could no longer be decided with words. England's king George III had already proclaimed the colonies in rebellion and issued orders to have the military put down the revolt. For its part, the Continental Congress had come to the conclusion that reconciliation was no longer an option now that British troops were on the march. The war that followed was the climax of the battle of wills and ideas that had preceded it. Neither side had given up their political or philosophical viewpoints; they simply translated their words into action.

CHRONOLOGY OF THE REVOLUTION

MARCH 1765

King George III of England approves the Stamp Act, which taxes the American colonies to help pay for the French and Indian War. Colonists protest the tax as unfair because it was levied without colonial representation in Parliament.

AUGUST 1768

Boston firebrand Samuel Adams calls for a boycott of English imports. In response, England sends troops to the colonies to maintain order.

MARCH 1770

Five colonists are killed after a brief confrontation with British soldiers outside Boston's Customs House. Known as the Boston Massacre, the event adds to the tensions in the colonies.

SEPTEMBER 1774

The colonies send delegates to the First Continental Congress to address the tensions between England and America.

JULY 1776

The Continental Congress votes to declare American independence. It adopts Thomas Jefferson's Declaration of Independence as its testimonial of British abuses and American resolve to be free.

DECEMBER 1776

Washington stages a daring surprise attack on Trenton, New Jersey, where Hessian mercenaries working for the British have camped for the winter.

OCTOBER 1777

While Washington fights battles in Pennsylvania, General Horatio Gates achieves a resounding victory over British general John Burgoyne's army near Saratoga, New York. Burgoyne's army is the first British command to surrender to patriot forces.

King George III of England

APRIL–AUGUST 1775

- The British commander in Boston sends units to nearby Lexington and Concord to seize colonial weapons and ammunition. The colonists are alerted to his move, and militia units from neighboring colonies converge on Concord to stop the British advance. The two sides exchange fire, and the British are forced to retreat back to Boston.

- The Continental Congress meets again to discuss breaking free from English rule. It appoints George Washington as the commander of military forces in America.

- Before Washington can arrive to take charge of the patriot units around Boston, the British advance and achieve a costly victory at the Battle of Bunker Hill.

- In August, after finally hearing of the skirmish at Lexington and Concord, King George III declares the colonies to be in revolt.

FEBRUARY 1778–JUNE 1779

- Benjamin Franklin helps broker a formal military alliance between France and America.

- France declares war on England.

- Spain officially declares war on England.

JULY–OCTOBER 1781

French troops arrive in Rhode Island. Their commander, the Comte de Rochambeau, persuades Washington to stage an offensive in the South against British forces under Lord Charles Cornwallis. With the French fleet cutting off Cornwallis's retreat by sea, the combined American and French armies surround the British army at Yorktown, Virginia, and force Cornwallis to surrender on October 19.

SEPTEMBER 1783

The Treaty of Paris is signed and the war ends, despite the fact that the Continental Congress would not finish ratifying the treaty until the following year. In November, George Washington resigns his commission as head of the Continental army.

George Washington

JAMES OTIS

No Taxation Without Representation

James Otis was a Boston lawyer who believed that people had certain rights—including life, liberty, and property—that were granted by God. In Otis's view, if a monarch or governing body infringes upon a citizen's God-given rights, then that citizen has the duty to demand a new government. In his well-known pamphlet, Rights of the British Colonies Asserted and Proved, *Otis argues that by instituting taxes in the American colonies—supposedly to pay for the costs of the recent French and Indian War—the English government is overstepping its bounds of authority. In order to be taxed, Otis insists, the colonists must agree to the tax and they must have a voice in the government that imposes the tax. According to Otis, the colonists have no representative in England's Parliament, and therefore any tax levied by England is unjust. Otis's pamphlet was written in 1765, a year after the passing of the Revenue Act (commonly known as the Sugar Act), which set taxes on goods such as sugar and coffee that entered colonial ports. Otis warns that if the colonists accept these taxes, more will surely follow.*

Boston lawyer
James Otis

Can there be any liberty where property is taken away without consent? Can it with any color of truth, justice, or equity be affirmed that the northern colonies are represented in Parliament? Has this whole continent of near three thousand miles in length, and in which and his other American dominions His Majesty has or very soon will have some millions of as good, loyal, and useful subjects, white and black. . . , the election of one member of the House of Commons?

Is there the least difference as to the consent of the colonists whether taxes and impositions are laid on their trade and other property by the crown alone or by the Parliament? . . . I can see no reason to doubt but the imposition of taxes, whether on trade, or on land, or houses, or ships, on real or personal, fixed or floating property, in the colonies is absolutely irreconcilable with the rights of the colonists as British subjects and as men. I say men, for in a state of nature no man can take my property from me without my consent: if he does, he deprives me of my liberty and makes me a slave. If such a proceeding is a breach of the law of nature, no law of

James Otis argued that the colonies should not be taxed because they were not represented in the British House of Commons (pictured).

society can make it just. The very act of taxing exercised over those who are not represented appears to me to be depriving them of one of their most essential rights as freemen, and if continued seems to be in effect an entire disfranchisement of every civil right. . . .

The sum of my argument is . . . that by [the British] constitution every man in the dominions is a free man; that no parts of His Majesty's dominions can be taxed without their consent; that every part has a right to be represented in the supreme or some subordinate legislature; that the refusal of this would seem to be a contradiction in practice to the theory of the constitution; that the colonies are subordinate dominions and are now in such a state as to make it best for the good of the whole that they should not only be continued in the enjoyment of subordinate legislation but be also represented in some proportion to their number and estates in the grand legislature of the nation; that this would firmly unite all parts of the British empire in the greater peace and prosperity, and render it invulnerable and perpetual.

James Otis, *Rights of the British Colonies Asserted and Proved*, 1765.

Glossary

- **equity:** fairness
- **affirmed:** declared
- **impositions:** burdens
- **floating:** movable
- **irreconcilable:** conflicting
- **disfranchisement:** stripping of rights
- **subordinate:** secondary
- **grand legislature:** Parliament
- **perpetual:** everlasting

WILLIAM PITT

Taxing America Is Unjust

> *William Pitt was a former prime minister of England when he joined the House of Lords (as the Earl of Chatham) in 1766. As a member of Parliament, Pitt became an outspoken critic of England's taxation of the American colonies. Because Pitt spoke up for the colonies, other members accused him of disloyalty to his king and his country. Pitt, however, believed the colonists, as British subjects, deserved representation in Parliament. In the following January 14, 1766, address to Parliament, Pitt argues for the repeal of the Stamp Act. He insists that the Americans have been treated unjustly by such taxes and that further injustices might jeopardize the economic relationship between the colonies and England.*

The gentleman [in Parliament who favors taxing the colonies] tells us of many who are taxed, and are not represented—The India Company, merchants, stockholders, manufacturers. Surely many of these are represented in other capacities, as owners of land, or as freemen of boroughs. It is a misfortune that more are not equally represented. But they are all inhabitants [of England], and as such, are they not virtually represented? Many have it in their option to be actually represented. They have connections with those that elect, and they have influence over them.

The gentleman asks: When were the colonies emancipated? But I desire to know when they were made slaves? But I dwell not upon words. . . . I will be bold to affirm that the profits to Great Britain from the trade of the colonies, through all its branches, is two millions a year. This is the fund that carried you triumphantly through the last war. The estates that were rented at two thousand pounds a year, threescore years ago, are at three thousand pounds at present. . . . This is the price America pays for her protection. . . . I dare not say how much higher these profits may be augmented. . . . I am convinced the commercial system of America may be altered to advantage. . . .

A great deal has been said without doors, of the power, of the strength of America. It is a topic that ought to be cautiously meddled with. In a good cause, on a sound bottom, the force of this country can crush America to atoms. I know the valor of your troops. I know the skill of your officers. There is not a company of foot that has served in America, out of which you may not pick a man of sufficient knowledge and experience to make a governor of a colony there. But on this ground, on the Stamp Act, when so many here will think it a crying injustice, I am one who will lift up my hands against it.

Members of Parliament accused William Pitt of disloyalty when he criticized England's taxation of the colonies.

Glossary

- **India Company:** a large British-run importing and exporting company
- **freemen of boroughs:** privileged voters in specific communities
- **emancipated:** freed from control
- **affirm:** state
- **the last war:** the French and Indian War
- **threescore:** sixty
- **without doors:** outside, in the streets
- **a sound bottom:** reasonable principle
- **foot:** foot soldiers, infantry
- **sheath:** put away (a sword or blade back into its scabbard)
- **prudence:** good sense
- **temper:** composure
- **occasioned:** brought about
- **undertake:** guarantee

In such a cause, your success would be hazardous. America, if she fell, would fall like the strong man. She would embrace the pillars of the state, and pull down the constitution along with her. Is this your boasted peace? Not to sheath the sword in its scabbard, but to sheath it in the bowels of your countrymen? . . . The Americans have not acted in all things with prudence and temper. The Americans have been wronged. They have been driven to madness by injustice. Will you punish them for the madness you have occasioned? Rather let prudence and temper come first from this side. I will undertake for America that she will follow the example.

Earl of Chatham, speech against the Stamp Act, given before Parliament, January 14, 1766.

PHILLIS WHEATLEY

Contradictions in the Right to Freedom

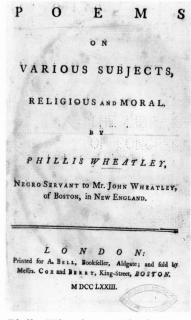

P O E M S

ON

VARIOUS SUBJECTS,

RELIGIOUS AND MORAL.

BY

PHILLIS WHEATLEY,

NEGRO SERVANT to Mr. JOHN WHEATLEY,
of BOSTON, in NEW ENGLAND.

L O N D O N:
Printed for A. BELL, Bookseller, Aldgate; and sold by
Messrs. COX and BERRY, King-Street, BOSTON.

M DCC LXXIII.

Phillis Wheatley was the first published African American poet. Her first collection was published in 1773 (pictured).

In 1761, seven-year-old Phillis Wheatley was sold as a slave to an educated Boston couple. The couple treated Wheatley well, and under their guidance, she learned to read and write. Wheatley began to write poetry. She had a few poems printed between 1767 and 1773, but in that latter year, while visiting England, she had her first collection published. When Wheatley and her owners returned to the colonies, Wheatley was set free. She was grateful, but chose to stay a few years with her former masters to care for them in their old age.

In February 1774, Wheatley wrote the following letter to the Reverend Samson Occom. Wheatley had been following the talk in the colonies about freedom from English tyranny. As a former slave, she was resentful that white patriots could argue that freedom was a God-given right while still holding so many blacks in slavery. Historians believe that on Occom's recommendation, Wheatley's letter was reprinted in several New England newspapers.

Though Wheatley received some fame as the first published African American poet, she died in poverty at the age of thirty-one.

Revered and honoured Sir, I have this day received your obliging kind epistle, and am greatly satisfied with your reasons respecting the negroes, and think highly reasonable what you offer in vindication of their natural rights: Those that invade them cannot be insensible that the divine light is chasing away the thick darkness which broods over the land of Africa; and the chaos which has reigned so long, is converting into beautiful order, and reveals more and more clearly the glorious dispensation of civil

Phillis Wheatley, a former slave, resented that white patriots fought for their own freedom while they kept blacks in slavery.

and religious liberty, which are so inseparably united, that there is little or no enjoyment of one without the other. . . . For in every human breast God has implanted a principle, which we call love of freedom; it is impatient of oppression, and pants for deliverance. . . . God grant deliverance in his own way and time, and get him honour upon all those [slaveholders] whose avarice impels them to countenance and help forward the calamities of their fellow creatures. This I desire not for their hurt, but to convince them of the strange absurdity of their conduct, whose words and actions are so diametrically opposite. How well the cry for liberty, and the reverse disposition for the exercise of oppressive power over others agree—I humbly think it does not require the penetration of a philosopher to determine.

Phillis Wheatley, letter to Samson Occom, February 11, 1774.

WILLIAM WIRT

Liberty or Death

In response to unfair taxation as well as abuses of authority, the colonial legislatures called together the First Continental Congress to draft a formal complaint to the British government. In 1774, the Congress decided to organize a boycott of English goods until King George III and Parliament agreed to resolve some of the problems that were driving England and the colonies apart. Not all Americans, however, were content with this strategy. In March 1775, Patrick Henry, one of the delegates to the Continental Congress, rose before the Virginia House of Burgesses—the colony's legislature—to declare why he believed any attempt to reconcile with England would only invite further abuse from the Crown.

William Wirt was in attendance at the House of Burgesses and recorded the audience's reaction to Henry's stirring call to arms.

Glossary

- **deputies:** representatives
- **grievances:** complaints
- **abject:** hopeless
- **solace:** comfort
- **comports:** conforms with
- **formidable:** powerful
- **adversary:** enemy
- **inevitable:** unavoidable

On Monday, the 20th of March, 1775, the convention of delegates, from the several counties and corporations of Virginia, met for the second time. . . . The reader will bear in mind the tone of the instructions given by the convention of the preceding year to their deputies in Congress. He will remember that, while they recite with great feeling the series of grievances under which the colonies had labored, and insist with firmness on their constitutional rights, they give, nevertheless, the most explicit and solemn pledge of their faith and true allegiance to his Majesty King George III. . . .

But Mr. Henry saw things with a steadier eye and a deeper insight. . . . He had long since read the true character of the British court, and saw that no alternative remained for his country but abject submission or heroic resistance. . . .

"He had," he said, "but one lamp by which his feet were guided; and that was the lamp of experience. He had no way of judging of the future but the past. And judging by the past, he wished to know what there had been in the conduct of the British ministry for the last ten years, to justify those hopes with which gentlemen had been pleased to solace themselves and the house? . . . Ask yourselves how this gracious reception of our petition comports with those warlike preparations which cover our waters and darken our land. Are fleets and armies necessary to a work of love and reconciliation? Have we shown ourselves so unwilling to be reconciled, that force must be called in to win back our love? Let us not deceive ourselves, sir. These are the implements of war and subjugation—the last arguments to which kings resort. . . .

"There is no longer any room for hope. If we wish to be free . . . we must fight!—I repeat it, sir, we must fight!! . . .

"They tell us, sir," continued Mr. Henry, "that we are weak—unable to cope with so formidable an adversary.

Patrick Henry, who believed it was no longer possible to negotiate with Britain, delivered an impassioned speech to the Virginia House of Burgesses in March 1775.

But when shall we be stronger. . . .Three millions of people armed in the holy cause of liberty and in such a country as that which we possess, are invincible by any force which our enemy can send against us. . . .There is no retreat but in submission and slavery! . . . The war is inevitable—and let it come!! I repeat it, sir, let it come!!!

". . . Gentlemen may cry, peace, peace—but there is no peace. The war is actually begun! The next gale that sweeps from the north will bring to our ears the clash of resounding arms! Our brethren are already in the field! Why stand we here idle? . . . Is life so dear, or peace so sweet, as to be purchased at the price of chains and slavery? Forbid it, Almighty God—I know not what course others may take; but as for me, . . . give me liberty, or give me death!"

He took his seat. No murmur of applause was heard. The effect was too deep. After the trance of a moment, several members started from their seats. The cry, "to arms!" seemed to quiver on every lip, and gleam from every eye.

William Wirt, *Sketches of the Life and Character of Patrick Henry.* Philadelphia: Claxton, 1818.

EDMUND BURKE

England Cannot Hope to Subdue the Colonies

In 1774, King George III officially proclaimed that the colonies were in a state of rebellion. He soon announced his plans to put down the rebellion by military force. Not all members of the king's government, however, agreed with this strategy. Edmund Burke, an Irish member of Parliament, believed that using force would never end the revolt. In a speech delivered on March 22, 1775, Burke reasoned that the Americans had the advantage in this contest. They were spirited, defending their home ground, and had the resources to prolong any fight. England, on the other hand, could not afford another long, costly war. Burke proposed that the colonies should be left to govern themselves under the English constitution, and he offered a peace plan to smooth over some of the recent misfortunes. Parliament, though, rejected the plan and prepared for war.

Edmund Burke tried to convince Parliament that Americans had the advantage in war because they were prepared to defend their home ground.

The proposition is peace. . . . I propose, by removing the ground of the difference, and by restoring the former unsuspecting confidence of the colonies in the mother country, to give permanent satisfaction to your people; and . . . to reconcile them to each other. . . .

America, gentlemen say, is . . . an object well worth fighting for. Certainly it is, if fighting a people be the best way of gaining them. . . . But I confess . . . my opinion is much more in favour of prudent management than of force. . . .

First . . . permit me to observe that the use of force alone is but temporary. It may subdue for a moment; but it does not remove the necessity of subduing again: and a nation is not governed, which is perpetually to be conquered. . . .

There is still . . . a consideration . . . which serves to determine my opinion. . . . I mean [America's] temper and character.

In this character of the Americans, a love of freedom is the predominating feature. . . . This fierce spirit of liberty is stronger in the English colonies probably than in any other people of the earth. . . .

Permit me . . . to add another circumstance in our colonies, which contributes . . . towards . . . this untractable spirit. I mean their education. In no country perhaps in the world is the law so general a study. . . .

This study renders men acute, inquisitive, dextrous, prompt in attack, ready in defence, full of resources. In other countries, the people, more simple, and of a less mercurial cast, judge of an ill principle in government only by an actual grievance; here they anticipate the evil, and judge of the pressure of the grievance by the badness of the principle. They . . . sniff the approach of tyranny in every tainted breeze.

The last cause of this disobedient spirit in the colonies is hardly less powerful than the rest . . . . Three thousand miles of ocean lie between you and them. . . . Seas roll, and months pass, between the order and the execution.

My idea, therefore . . . is to admit the people of our colonies into an interest in the constitution; and, by recording that admission in the journals of Parliament, to give them as strong an assurance as the nature of the thing will admit, that we mean forever to adhere to that solemn declaration of systematic indulgence.

Edmund Burke, "On Conciliation with America," speech before Parliament, March 22, 1775.

Glossary

- **unsuspecting:** unquestioning
- **reconcile:** reunite
- **prudent:** sensible
- **perpetually:** continually
- **predominating:** major
- **contributes:** adds
- **untractable:** intractable, stubborn
- **general a study:** widely studied
- **renders:** makes
- **acute:** sharp
- **inquisitive:** curious
- **dextrous:** dexterous, skillful
- **mercurial cast:** erratic attitude
- **grievance:** complaint
- **the order and the execution:** saying and doing
- **admit the people. . . into an interest in the constitution:** allow the people to take part in their own government
- **solemn:** formal
- **systematic indulgence:** regular tolerance

LORD JOHN DUNMORE

A Proclamation Offering Freedom to the Slaves

Lord John Dunmore, the royally appointed governor of Virginia, feared for the safety of the British loyalists in his colony when war broke out in April 1775. Most British troops in the southern colonies had been sent north to support Boston, the center of the fighting. With only three hundred British soldiers left under his command, Dunmore decided to recruit slaves into his army. To this end, Dunmore issued one of the most provocative orders of the day. In his proclamation, excerpted below, Dunmore offered freedom to all black slaves who fled their rebel masters and agreed to fight in the British army. Many Virginians were outraged at this decree. Slaveholders lived with the fear that their slaves would rise against them, but in this case, the British were willing to arm the slaves with muskets.

Five hundred African Americans offered their services within a week. Dunmore formed them into the Ethiopia Regiment and gave the recruits guns and uniforms as fast as they arrived. To try to stem the tide of fleeing slaves, rebel newspapers begged blacks to remain loyal to the patriot cause. Many blacks, however, recognized that the patriots' cry for freedom did not extend to the slaves.

196

NEW-YORK, 21st April 1783.

THIS is to certify to whomsoever it may concern, that the Bearer hereof *Cato Ramsay* a Negro, resorted to the British Lines, in consequence of the Proclamations of Sir William Howe, and Sir Henry Clinton, late Commanders in Chief in America; and that the said Negro has hereby his Excellency Sir Guy Carleton's Permission to go to Nova-Scotia, or wherever else he may think proper.

By Order of Brigadier General Birch,

Slaves who left their owners and joined the British army received certificates of freedom (pictured) for their service.

As I have ever entertained hopes that an accommodation might have taken place between Great Britain and this colony, without being compelled by my duty to do this most disagreeable, but now absolutely necessary duty, rendered so by a body of men, unlawfully assembled, firing on his majesty's tenders, and the formation of an army, and an army now on its march to attack his majesty's troops, and destroy the well disposed subjects of this colony. To defeat such treasonable purposes, and that all such traitors, and their abettors may be brought to justice, and that the peace and good order of this colony may be again restored . . . I have thought fit to issue this my proclamation, hereby declaring that . . . I do, in virtue of the power and authority to me given, by his majesty, determine to execute martial law, and cause the same to be executed throughout this colony; and to the end that peace and good order may the sooner be restored, I do require every person capable of bearing arms to resort to his majesty's standard, or be looked upon as traitors to his majesty's crown and government, and thereby become liable to the penalty the law inflicts upon such offences; such as forfeiture of life, confiscation of lands, etc., etc. And I do hereby further declare all indentured servants, negroes, or others . . . free, that are able and willing to bear arms, they joining his majesty's troops as soon as may be, for the more speedily reducing his colony to a proper sense of their duty to his majesty's crown and dignity.

Glossary

- **entertained:** gave thought to
- **accommodation:** beneficial change
- **compelled:** forced
- **rendered:** made
- **tenders:** supply boats
- **well disposed:** good intentioned, loyal
- **abettors:** assistants
- **martial law:** military rule
- **arms:** weapons
- **resort to his majesty's standard:** join under the British flag
- **liable:** legally responsible
- **forfeiture of life:** loss of one's life, to death or imprisonment
- **confiscation:** taking away
- **indentured servants:** poor whites who sell themselves into servitude

Lord John Dunmore, Proclamation Freeing the Slaves, November 1775.

THOMAS PAINE

Common Sense

By 1776, the first shots of the Revolution had been fired, but many colonists were still unsure whether war was the correct way to resolve their differences with England. Thomas Paine was not one of those harboring doubts. Although he was the son of an English Quaker, Paine was not hesitant to support armed resistance when colonial liberties were threatened. In his widely read pamphlet, Common Sense—*published anonymously in January 1776—Paine insisted that America should be independent from England. This desire for independence, he argued, should not spring from a dislike of English taxes, but rather from a rejection of the tyrannical manner in which the colonies had been bullied and enslaved. Paine even argued that independence would be in the best interests of both America and England since Britain's chief interest in the colonies was commercial and America had no better trading partner than England. In the following excerpt from* Common Sense, *Paine concludes by imploring all Americans—Whigs (those dissatisfied with English rule), Tories (those still loyal to England), and the undecided—to pull together and build a new, independent nation founded on the principles of freedom.*

The taking up arms merely to enforce the repeal of a pecuniary law seems as unwarrantable by the divine law and as repugnant to human feelings as the taking up arms to enforce the obedience thereto. The object, on either side, does not justify the means; for the lives of men are too valuable to be cast away on such trifles. It is the violence which is done and threatened to our persons; the destruction of our property by an armed force; the invasion of our country by fire and sword, which conscientiously qualifies the use of arms: And the instant in which such a mode of defense became necessary, all subjection to Britain ought to have ceased, and the independency of America should have been considered as dating its era from, and published by, the first musket that was fired against her. This line is a line of consistency neither drawn by caprice nor extended by ambition, but produced by a chain of events of which the colonies were not the authors. . . .

In short, independence is the only bond that can tie and keep us together. We shall then see our object, and our ears will be legally shut against the schemes of an intriguing, as well as a cruel enemy. We shall then too be on a proper footing to treat with Britain; for there is reason to conclude that the pride of that court will be less hurt by treating with the American states for terms of peace than with those she

Thomas Paine urged all Americans to unite and win independence.

denominates "rebellious subjects," for terms of accommodation. It is our delaying it that encourages her to hope for conquest, and our backwardness tends only to prolong the war. . . .
Instead of gazing at each other with suspicious or doubtful curiosity, let each of us hold out to his neighbor the hearty hand of friendship, and unite in drawing a line, which, like an act of oblivion, shall bury in forgetfulness every former dissension. Let the names of Whig and Tory be extinct; and let none other be heard among us than those of a good citizen, an open and resolute friend, and a virtuous supporter of the rights of mankind and of the free and independent states of America.

Thomas Paine, *Common Sense*, January 1776.

SAMUEL HOPKINS

A Message to Slaveholders

Samuel Hopkins was a Congregationalist minister in Rhode Island when the Revolutionary War broke out. He was a supporter of the patriot cause, but his chief concerns were with social evils such as the ongoing slave trade in the colonies. While in Rhode Island, Hopkins had observed the cruelty of the slave trade first-

Samuel Hopkins addressed the contradiction in a fight for freedom by those who owned slaves.

hand, and, believing the enslavement of any person was a sin, he began preaching and writing against slavery in America.

In 1776, Hopkins wrote A Dialogue Concerning the Slavery of the Africans. *This pamphlet took the form of an imaginary dialogue in which two people discuss the morality of slavery. Throughout, Hopkins uses logic as well as religious doctrine to condemn slavery and the slave trade as unjust and immoral. At the end of his pamphlet, Hopkins added a special message to slave-holders and members of the Continental Congress, both of whom, Hopkins argues, have the power to set the nation's slaves free. In this postscript, excerpted below, Hopkins explains how "inconsistent" it is for colonists to clamor for their own freedom while still holding blacks in bondage.*

Gentlemen, . . . It would be injurious, it is confessed, to consider you as the only persons guilty or concerned in this matter. The several legislatures in these colonies, the magistrates, and the body of the people have doubtless been greatly guilty in approving & encouraging, or at least conniving at this practice. Yea, every one is in a measure guilty who has been inattentive to this oppression, and unaffected with it, and neglected to bear proper testimony against it, and do all in his power to put a stop to it. And it is granted the public ought to go into some effectual measures to liberate all the slaves, without laying an unreasonable burden on their masters. But tho' this be not done, such neglect will not excuse you in holding them in slavery, as it is in your power to set them free, and your indispensable duty, and really your interest, to do them this piece of justice, tho' others should neglect to assist you as they ought.

It is hoped you will not be offended with the plainness of speech used on this subject; and that, tho' you should at first think some of the epithets and expressions which are used, too severe, and find the subject itself disagreeable, this will not prevent your attentively considering it . . . with the utmost impartiality and readiness to receive conviction, how much soever you may find yourselves condemned. . . . And is it not worthy your serious consideration that they who are not interested in this practice, and have no slaves, are generally, if not every one, fully convinced it is wrong? Are they not, at least many of them, as capable of judging in this matter as you yourselves are; and therefore more likely to judge right than you as they are uninterested and impartial? The conviction of the unjustifiableness of this practice has been increasing, and greatly spread of late; and many who have had slaves have found themselves so unable to justify their own conduct in holding them in bondage, as to be induced to set them at liberty. May this conviction soon reach every owner of slaves in North-America!

To this end you are desired to consider. . . . the very inconsistent part you act, while you are thus enslaving your fellow men, and yet condemning and strenuously opposing those who are attempting to bring you and your children into a state of bondage, much lighter than that in which you keep your slaves; who yet have at least as good a right to make slaves of you and your children, as you have to hold your brethren in this state of bondage. Men do not love to be inconsistent with themselves: and therefore this is so evident and glaring, that if you will only suffer yourselves to reflect a moment, it must give you pain from which you can find no relief but by freeing your slaves or relinquishing the cause of public liberty, which you have thought so glorious and worthy to be pursued at the risk of your fortunes and lives.

Glossary

- **injurious:** insulting
- **it is confessed:** I admit
- **magistrates:** judges
- **conniving:** scheming
- **to bear proper testimony:** speak out
- **effectual:** effective
- **indispensable:** required
- **ought:** should
- **plainness:** directness
- **epithets:** labels
- **impartiality:** fairness
- **conviction:** a guilty verdict
- **unjustifiableness:** indefensibleness
- **of late:** recently
- **induced:** persuaded
- **part:** role
- **strenuously:** strongly
- **suffer:** allow
- **reflect:** think
- **relinquishing:** giving up

Samuel Hopkins, *A Dialogue Concerning the Slavery of the Africans,* 1776.

SAMUEL ADAMS

We Have No Other Alternative than Independence

Samuel Adams was a Boston politician and an outspoken champion of American independence. His vocal opposition to Parliament's "interference" in the colonies was well known to the British, who considered Adams a dangerous nuisance. Adams also served as a delegate to the Continental Congress, where he continually argued for separation from Britain rather than trying to make amends.

When the Second Continental Congress ratified the Declaration of Independence, Adams took to the streets to explain the significance of the document to the public. In the following excerpt from a speech delivered at the State House in Philadelphia, Pennsylvania, on August 1, 1776, Adams preaches the virtues of independence.

The doctrine of dependence on Great Britain is, I believe, generally exploded; but as I would attend to the honest weakness of the simplest of men, you will pardon me if I offer a few words on that subject.

We are now on this continent, to the astonishment of the world, three millions of souls united in one cause. We have large armies, well disciplined and appointed, with commanders inferior to none in military skill, and superior in activity and zeal. We are furnished with arsenals and stores beyond our most sanguine expectations, and foreign nations are waiting to crown our success by their alliances. There are instances of, I would say, an almost astonishing providence in our favor; our success has staggered our enemies, and almost given faith to infidels; so we may truly say it is not our own arm which has saved us. . . .

If there is any man so base or so weak as to prefer a dependence on Great Britain to the dignity and happiness of living a member of a free and independent nation, let me tell him that necessity now demands what the generous principle of patriotism should have dictated.

We have no other alternative than independence, or the most ignominious and galling servitude. The legions of our enemies thicken on our plains; desolation and death mark their bloody career, while the mangled corpses of our countrymen seem to cry out to us as a voice from Heaven. . . .

You have now in the field armies sufficient to repel the whole force of your enemies and their base and mercenary auxiliaries. The hearts of your soldiers beat high with the spirit of freedom; they are animated with the justice of their cause, and

Samuel Adams (left) was a vocal opponent of British involvement in the colonies who argued for independence rather than reconciliation.

Glossary

- **doctrine:** policy
- **exploded:** proved wrong
- **zeal:** enthusiasm
- **furnished:** provided
- **arsenals:** weapons storehouses
- **sanguine:** optimistic
- **providence:** divine luck
- **infidels:** nonbelievers
- **base:** lowly
- **ignominious:** shameful
- **galling:** irritating
- **desolation:** misery
- **mercenary auxiliaries:** hired soldiers, referring to the German troops hired by Britain
- **adversaries:** enemies
- **derision:** mockery
- **enterprise:** undertaking

while they grasp their swords can look up to Heaven for assistance. Your adversaries are composed of wretches who laugh at the rights of humanity, who turn religion into derision, and would, for higher wages, direct their swords against their leaders or their country. Go on, then, in your generous enterprise with gratitude to Heaven for past success, and confidence of it in the future. For my own part I ask no greater blessing than to share with you the common danger and common glory.

Samuel Adams, speech given before the Pennsylvania State House, August 1, 1776.

THOMAS JEFFERSON

The Declaration of Independence

In June 1776, the Continental Congress was called into session for a second time. The assembled delegates had to determine how they would finance and conduct a war now that one was upon them. They also had to draft some formal document that would proclaim America's immediate separation from Britain. Thomas Jefferson, a lawyer and delegate from Virginia, was given the task of writing the Declaration of Independence. Jefferson worked quickly and went through a few drafts. When he submitted the work for the approval of the Second Continental Congress, the various delegates made several alterations and cuts. Benjamin Franklin tried to raise Jefferson's spirits as his words were deleted or changed, but Jefferson sat silently throughout the ordeal. He never publicly challenged the changes made to his original document, but privately he believed his words had been "mutilated" by the Congress.

On July 4, 1776, Congress voted whether to accept the altered document or not. The debate lasted long into the evening. Finally, all colonies except New York endorsed the Declaration of Independence. Five days later, the New York delegation ratified the document after getting approval from their colonial government. Copies of the declaration were sent out to newspapers, colonial officials, and military commanders on July 5. Soon all of colonial America received word that the union between England and its colonies was dissolved. The reasons why the colonists believed themselves justified in dissolving that union are eloquently laid out in the opening paragraph of the declaration.

When in the Course of human events, it becomes necessary for one people to dissolve the political bands which have connected them with another, and to assume among the Powers of the earth, the separate and equal station to which the Laws of Nature and of Nature's God entitle them, a decent respect to the opinions of mankind requires that they should declare the causes which impel them to the separation.

We hold these truths to be self-evident, that all men are created equal, that they are endowed by their Creator with certain unalienable Rights, that among these are Life, Liberty and the pursuit of Happiness. That to secure these rights, Governments are instituted among Men, deriving their just powers from the consent of the governed, That whenever any Form of Government becomes destructive of these ends,

Thomas Jefferson worked tirelessly to draft the document that declared America's complete independence from England.

Jefferson's words expressed the basic ideals at the heart of America's fight for independence.

it is the Right of the People to alter or to abolish it, and to institute new Government, laying its foundation on such principles and organizing its powers in such form, as to them shall seem most likely to effect their Safety and Happiness. Prudence, indeed, will dictate that Governments long established should not be changed for light and transient causes; and accordingly all experience hath shown, that mankind are more disposed to suffer, while evils are sufferable, than to right themselves by abolishing the forms to which they are accustomed. But when a long train of abuses and usurpations, pursuing invariably the same Object, evinces a design to reduce them under absolute Despotism, it is their right, it is their duty, to throw off such Government, and to provide new Guards for their future security.—Such has been the patient sufferance of these Colonies; and such is now the necessity which constrains them to alter their former Systems of Government. The history of the present King of Great Britain is a history of repeated injuries and usurpations, all having in direct object the establishment of an absolute Tyranny over these States. To prove this, let Facts be submitted to a candid world.

Thomas Jefferson, Declaration of Independence, July 4, 1776.

FOR MORE INFORMATION

Books

Sam Fink, *The Declaration of Independence*. New York: Scholastic Reference, 2002.

Dennis Brindell Fradin, *Samuel Adams: The Father of American Independence*. New York: Clarion, 1998.

————, *The Signers: The Fifty-Six Stories Behind the Declaration of Independence*. New York: Walker, 2002.

Stuart Kallen, *Patrick Henry*. Edina, MN: Abdo, 1999.

Web Sites

The History Place: The American Revolution
www.historyplace.com
One of the many topics covered by The History Place Web site, this series of pages on the Revolution presents time lines of the era. On each time line page, visitors can access information that relates to the period between early colonization and 1790.

Kid Info: American Revolution
www.kidinfo.com
This Web site gathers links to other sites devoted to some aspect of the Revolution. This is a good place to track down further information on a specific topic of interest.

Liberty: The American Revolution
www.pbs.org
A companion to the PBS documentary miniseries on the Revolution, this Web site is an excellent resource for students.

INDEX